W9-AHY-714

Confessions to My Mother

Other books by Cathy Guisewite

I Am Woman, Hear Me Snore

Abs of Steel, Buns of Cinnamon

Understanding the "Why" Chromosome

*The Child Within Has Been Awakened but
the Old Lady on the Outside Just Collapsed*

Revelations from a 45-Pound Purse

*Only Love Can Break a Heart,
But a Shoe Sale Can Come Close*

$14 in the Bank and a $200 Face in My Purse

My Granddaughter Has Fleas!

*Why Do the Right Words Always Come Out
of the Wrong Mouth?*

A Hand to Hold, an Opinion to Reject

Thin Thighs in Thirty Years

Wake Me Up When I'm a Size 5

Men Should Come with Instruction Booklets

A Mouthful of Breath Mints and No One to Kiss

Another Saturday Night of Wild and Reckless Abandon

Cathy Twentieth Anniversary Collection

Reflections: A Fifteenth Anniversary Collection

Confessions to My Mother

Cathy Guisewite

**Andrews McMeel
Publishing**

Kansas City

8803298

Confessions to My Mother copyright © 1999 by Cathy Guisewite. All rights reserved. Printed in the United States of America. No part of this book may be used or reproduced in any manner whatsoever without written permission except in the case of reprints in the context of reviews. For information, write Andrews McMeel Publishing, an Andrews McMeel Universal company, 4520 Main Street, Kansas City, Missouri 64111.

99 00 01 02 03 RDC 10 9 8 7 6 5 4 3 2 1

www.andrewsmcmeel.com

Library of Congress Cataloging-in-Publication Data

Guisewite, Cathy.
     Confessions to my mother / Cathy Guisewite.
          p.   cm.
     ISBN 0-8362-8788-6 (hardcover)
     1. Mothers and daughters—Humor.   2. Mothers and daughters—
—Cartoons and caricatures.   I. Title.
PN6726.G85   1999
741.5'973—dc21   99-11624
                                                                        CIP

———————— ATTENTION: SCHOOLS AND BUSINESSES ————————

Andrews McMeel books are available at quantity discounts with bulk purchase for educational, business, or sales promotional use. For information, please write to: Special Sales Department, Andrews McMeel Publishing, 4520 Main Street, Kansas City, Missouri 64111.

To Mom

Confessions
to My Mother

I have never thrown a towel
on the floor in my life
without hearing your voice.

I've always needed
your approval the most
and believed
your compliments the least.

In the thousands of hours
I spent by your side
watching you cook,
the only thing I learned
how to do was taste things.

Every dream I've had
for myself was to help you finish
a dream I thought
you had for yourself.

When you're not there,
I order the exact same thing
for dinner that you would.

You are the bravest person
I ever met.

Without looking in the mirror,
I can tell when my face has an
expression exactly like yours.

I can no longer read
a newspaper without a pair
of scissors in my hand.

Even when you're
nowhere near me,
you always cast a vote.

⚜————♥————⚜

I've started eating the
heels of the bread.

After a lifetime of ridiculing you for it, I now also have a section in my closet of "clothes that are too nice to wear."

Because of you, I can't throw out a cardboard box.

Because of you, I also can't throw out a ribbon, a bow, a piece of gift wrap, a piece of bubble wrap, a cardboard tube, an envelope, or a free sample of anything.

Because of you,
I rent storage space.

Because of you, I always buy
special desserts to have on
hand for company, store them
in the freezer, and then eat them
frozen solid.

I wish I hadn't moved so far away from home.

Even when it's been months
since I last saw you, I can still
feel the exact outline of
your body hugging mine,
and the exact shape of
your face in my hand.

Part of me is still hoping
to grow up and be you.

Nothing anyone has ever said
to me matches the power of
one look from you.

When something great or terrible happens to me, you aren't always the first person I tell, but you're always the first person I think of.

I was in my twenties before it occurred to me that you were a regular human being, not some different Motherhood species.

The things you've blown have been as inspiring to me as the things you've succeeded at.

I not only inherited the "fat gene" from you, but the "disorganized-photo-album gene."

MISC.
PHOTOS AND
NEGATIVES

MISC.
PHOTOS AND
NEGATIVES

I always open mail
I get from you first.

Your twenty-four-hour motherly hotline means more to me than Call Waiting, Call Forwarding, Caller ID, and voice mail combined.

You are the worst person
in the history of the universe
to clean a closet with.

I have always thought
you are the most beautiful
woman in the world.

Even though I've ignored your free
  advice all my life, I've paid:
a nutritionist to tell me to eat my
  vegetables . . .
a trainer to tell me to exercise . . .
a chiropractor to tell me to quit
  slouching . . .
a financial adviser to tell me to save
  some money . . .
and a therapist to tell me I'm a
  wonderful human being who can
  do anything I set my mind to.

You were right about
"what's his name."

You were right about the
eyebrow-plucking thing.

You were also right about the multiple-piercing thing, the tattoo thing, the hair-dying thing, the no-bra thing, the dental floss thing, the vitamin thing, and the baby-oil-as-suntan-lotion thing.

Whenever my friends
and I talk about mothers,
you always win.

I've bought clothes just to spite you, worn them to horrify you, and then blamed you for the fact that I'm not only always in debt, but I'm also always wearing the wrong thing.

I love that you can't even go
into a gas station snack shop
without browsing.

♡

I love that you never ask what happened to the hundreds of articles of clothing that we spent thousands of hours choosing, altering, trying on, discussing, and coordinating.

The inside of my bathroom cabinet looks exactly as bad as the inside of your bathroom cabinet.

Almost nothing is as touching to me as remembering how enthusiastic and open-minded you tried to be about all my doomed relationships.

All the time I've been looking for a man who's worthy of me, I've also been looking for a man who's worthy of you.

⚬————♥————⚬

I sometimes spend all day thinking about how much I miss you, and then snap at you the second I hear your voice on the phone.

When I make your chicken soup, it doesn't taste like your chicken soup.

Every piece of your advice that
I've rejected I've now
given to someone else.

I'm sorry for the ten to fifteen years that I spent grunting at you.

Even though you know me
better than anyone in the world,
I still clean the house before you
come as though I were trying to
impress a complete stranger.

The fact that you have such a
good relationship with God has
always made me feel very safe.

Because of you, I know how to
write a perfect thank-you note,
and because of that,
my thank-you notes are
always late.

I know I've given you lots of
wrinkles but, through the miracle
of genetics, you've already
given some of them right back.

❀————♥————❀

I'm so proud of how much
everyone loves you.

It's equally inspiring and
depressing to me that you have
basically the same "To Do" piles
on your desk that you've had
since I was born.

No one I've ever met in my
life can make me as crazy
as quickly as you can.

I do things exactly the way you do them, even when you've quit doing them that way.

Almost everything I ate
between the ages of
eighteen and twenty-eight
I blamed on you.

❦

It's easier for me to pay the woman behind the cosmetics counter $250 than to admit that your 29-cent moisturizer works.

———— ♡ ————

The sweetest things you
do for me are some of
the most annoying.

The thing I am the most sure of
in my life is that you love me.

The times I notice I'm most
like you are when I'm doing
something incredibly nice
for someone.

My memories of sitting and eating something fattening with you are so much deeper and richer than my memories of sitting and eating something nonfattening with you.

When you're not here,
I'm as cheap as you are.

Of all the hairdos and clothes
and looks and sizes and ages
you've been through the years,
I have one precise picture
of you in my mind that
never varies.

I wish I could live one day
over with you when I was
five, ten, fifteen, and
twenty years old.

I sometimes wake up in the middle of the night tortured with guilt about all the money you spent on me.

Until very recently, it never even occurred to me that you could be insecure about something.

If I'd had any idea how hard it is to be a parent, I would have been way nicer to you.

After the thousands of dollars
you spent making sure I got
to see the world, the only place
I actually care about being
is in your kitchen.

The fact that you're with me twenty-four hours a day from 3,000 miles away gives me great comfort that you'll always be with me. How much farther away could heaven be than Florida?